Flower Coloring
Book
For Adults

FLOWER COLORING

SOCIAL MEDIA

f /MySweetBooks1

/MySweetBooks1

/MySweetBooks1

/MySweetBooks

Email Us : mysweetbooks1@gmail.com

Mother

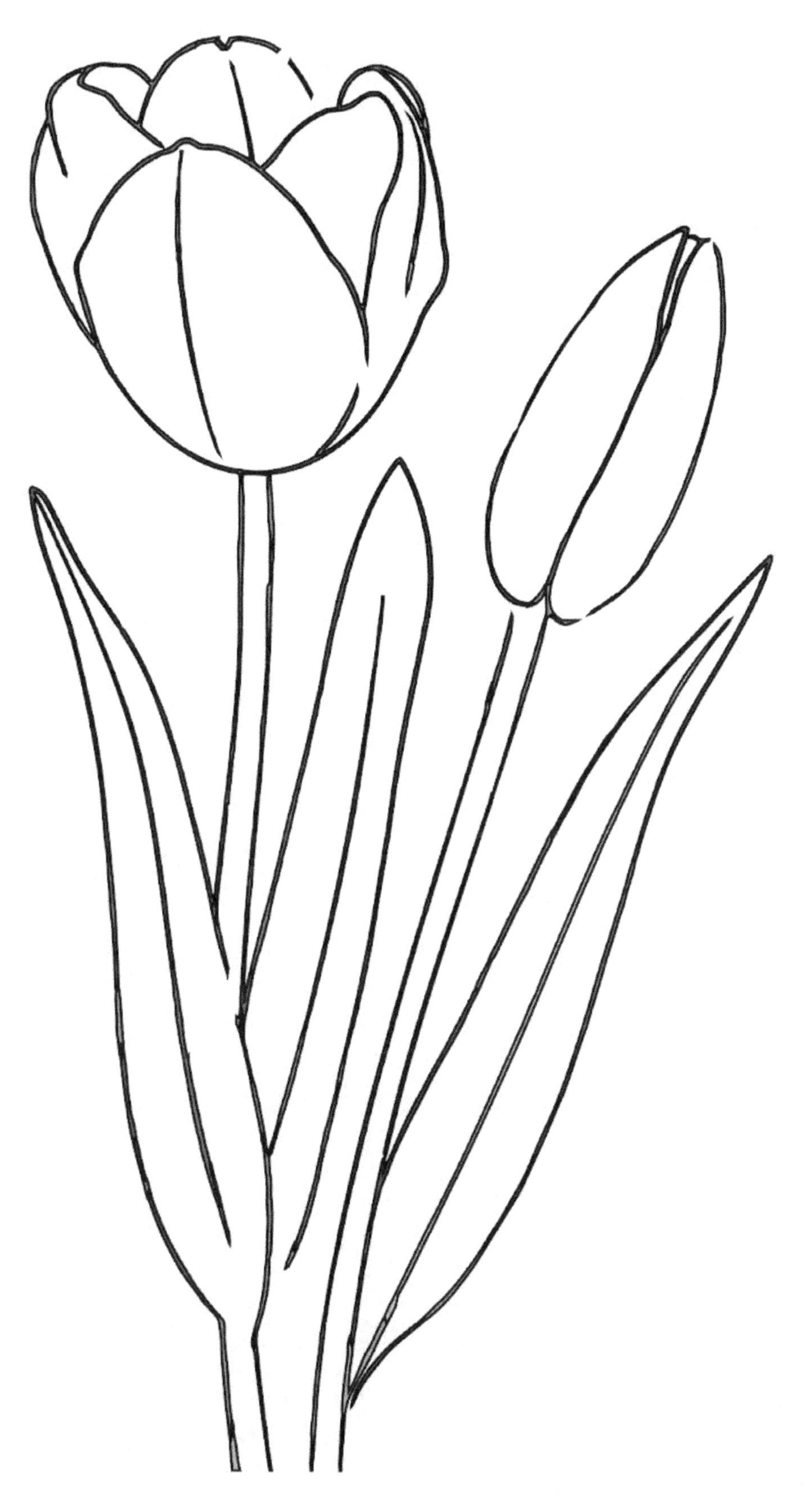

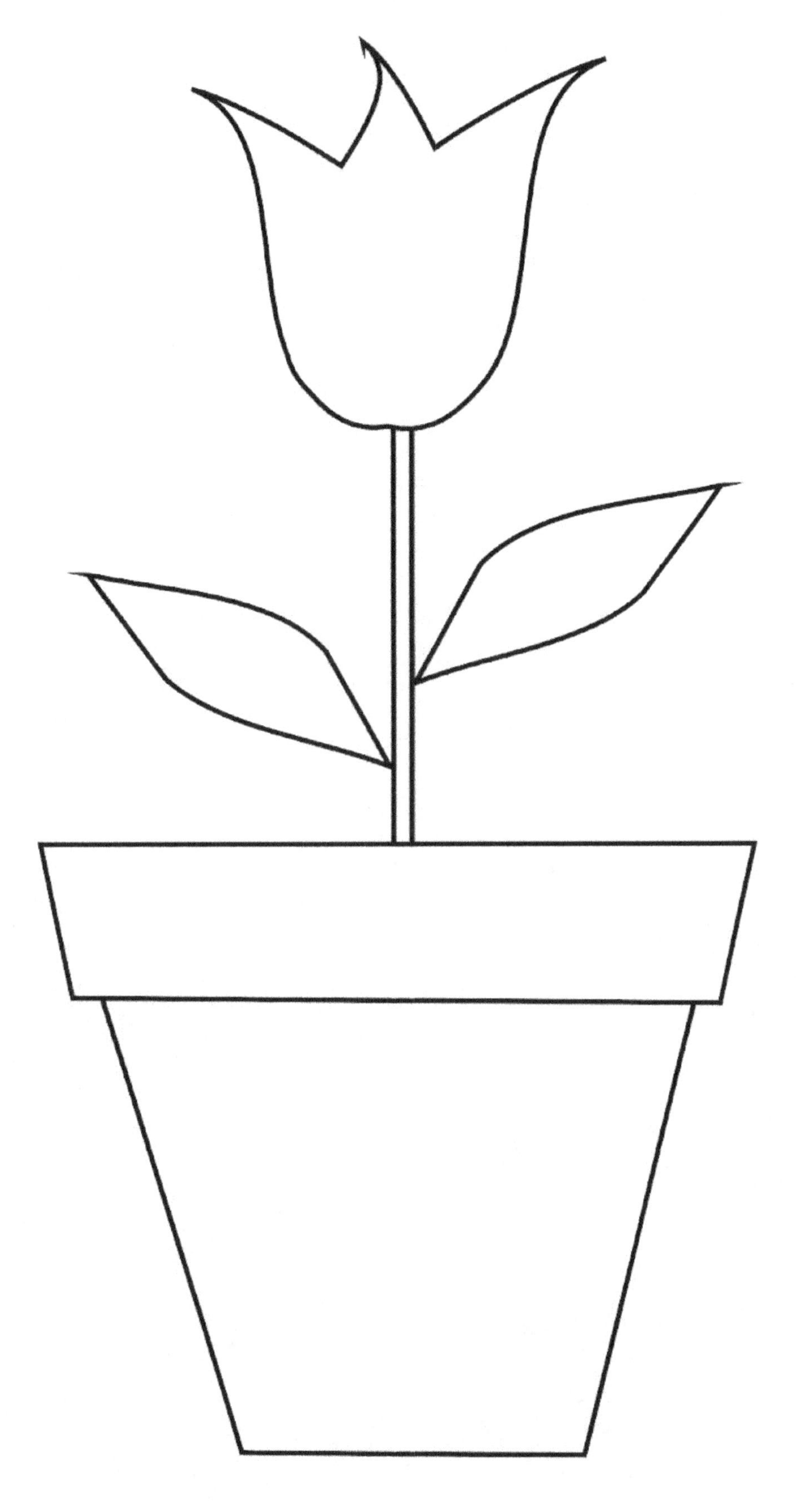

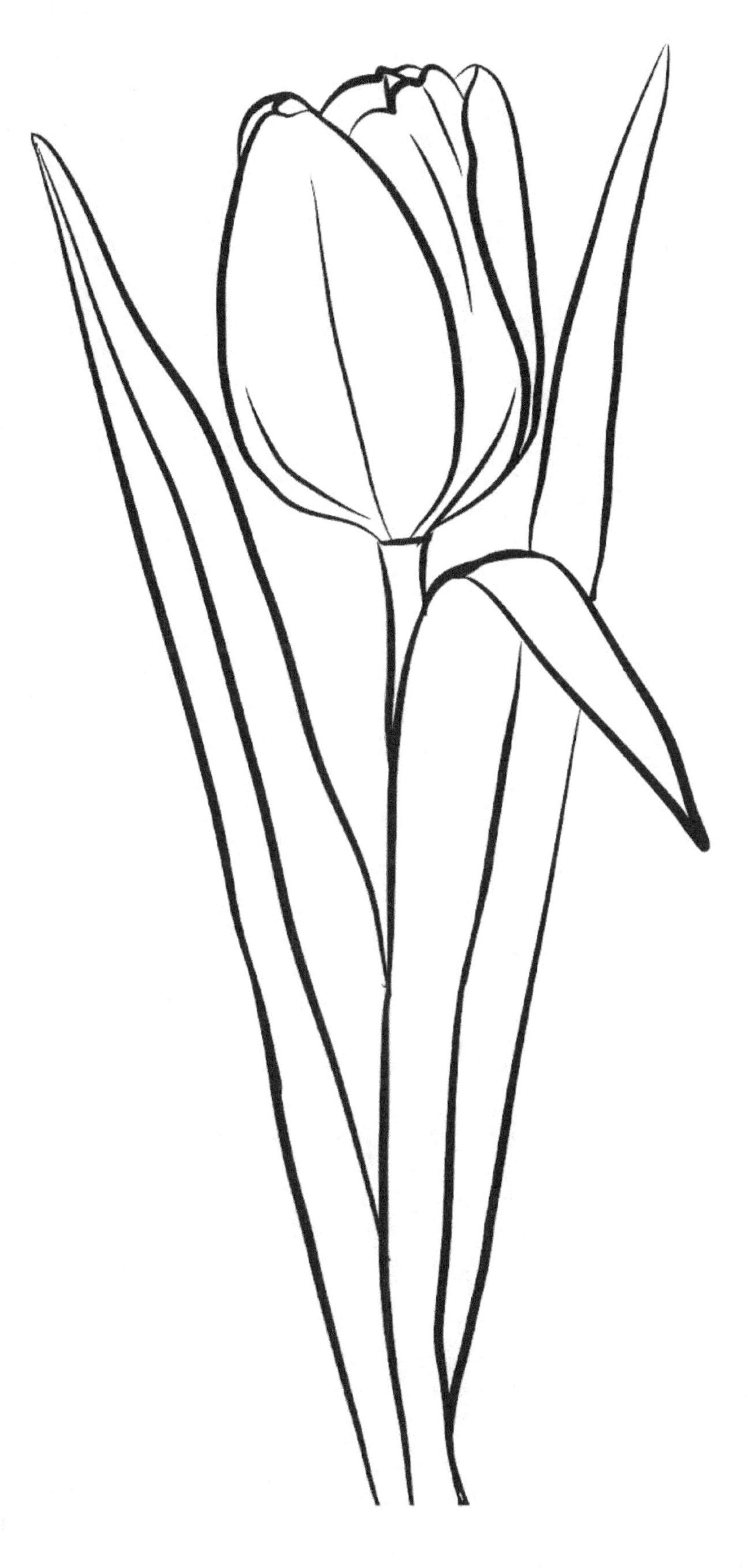

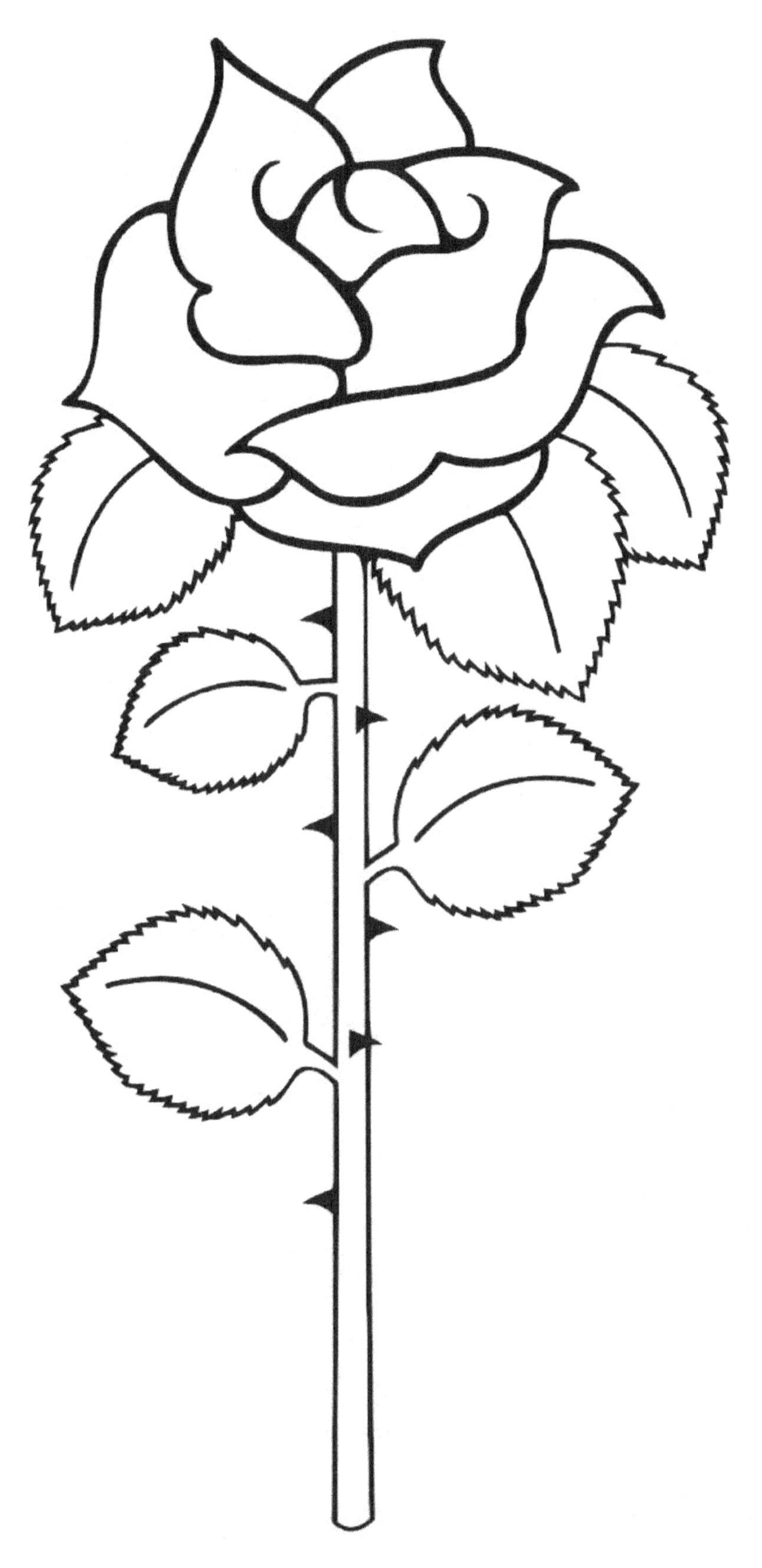

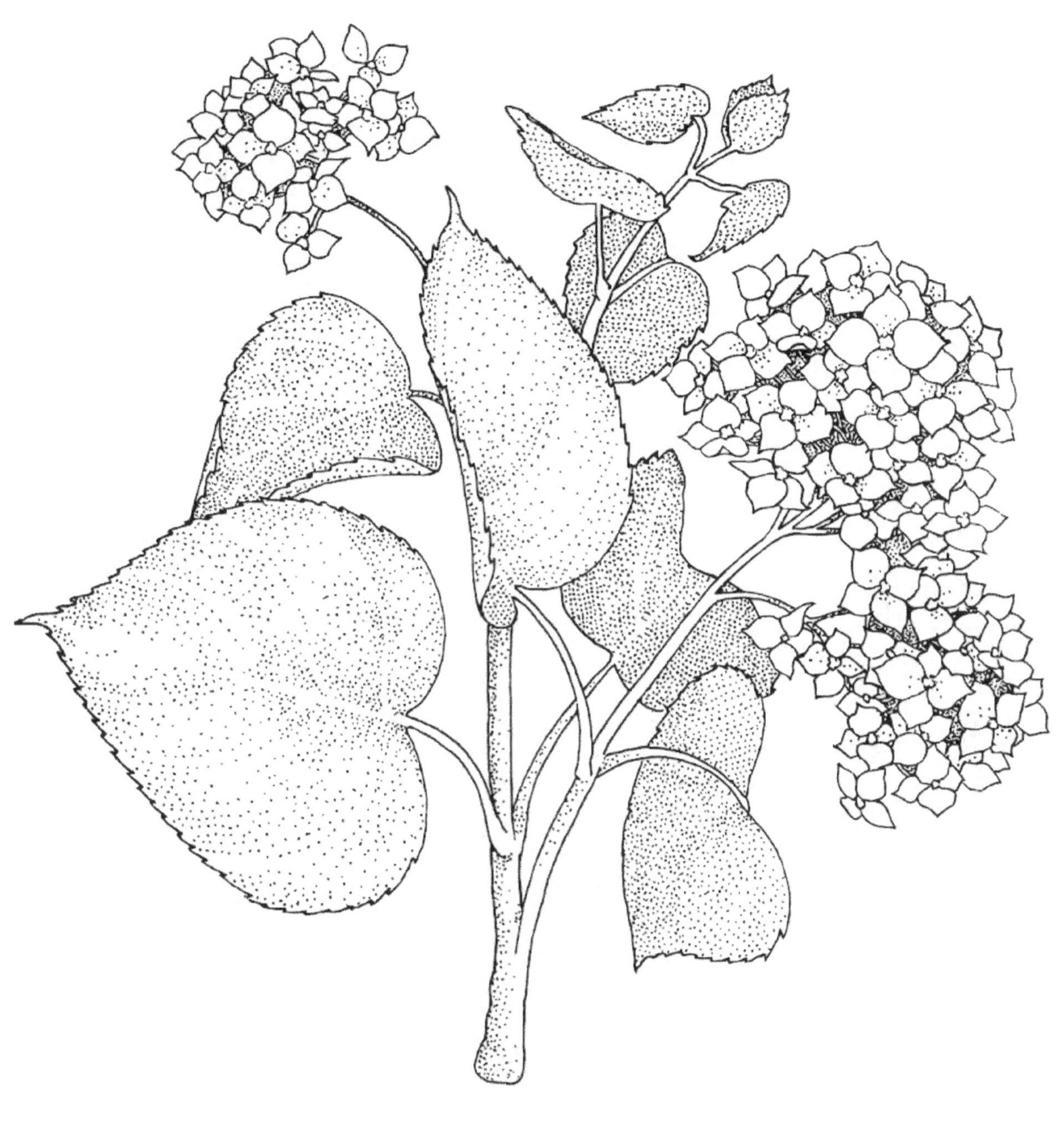

9 781670 703200